OTHER-WORDly

words both strange and lovely
from around the world

by **YEE-LUM MAK**   *illustrated by* **KELSEY GARRITY-RILEY**

chronicle books san francisco

OTHER-WORDLY started when I stumbled across the Portuguese word *saudade*: "the love that remains"; a longing for someone or something that you had loved and then lost.

I'd never seen anything like it before. It seemed other-worldly: bigger, stranger, and fuller than the words we use every day. It was a word for a feeling I'd felt, but had never been able to name. If there were more words like that, I wanted to find them.

And when I started looking, I found that every language has names for the odd and wonderful, for the unexpected things that have meaning, for the parts of our lives that are "other-wordly."

GÖKOTTA (noun, n, Swedish)

*lit. "dawn picnic to hear the first birdsong"; the act of rising
in the early morning to watch the birds or to go
outside to appreciate nature*

KOMOREBI (noun, Japanese)

the sunlight that filters through the leaves of the trees

JENTACULAR (adjective, English)

having to do with an early breakfast

KUMMERSPECK (noun, m, German)

excessive weight gained through eating

as a means of relieving stress or strong emotion

BRUMOUS (adjective, English)
of gray skies and winter days; filled with heavy clouds or fog; relating to winter or cold, sunless weather

BRONTIDE (noun, English)
the low rumble, as of distant thunder

NEFELIBATA (noun, m+f, Spanish and Portuguese)

lit. "cloud-walker"; one who lives in the clouds of their own imagination or dreams, or one who does not obey the conventions of society, literature, or art

HOPPÍPOLLA (verb phr., Icelandic)

jumping into puddles

TATEMAE (noun, Japanese)

what a person pretends to believe; the behavior and opinions
one must display to satisfy society's demands

HONNE (noun, Japanese)

what a person truly believes; the behavior and opinions that are
often kept hidden and only displayed with one's closest confidants

ONIOCHALASIA (noun, English)

buying or shopping as a method of stress relief or relaxation

TSUNDOKU (noun, Japanese)

*buying books and not reading them; letting books pile
up unread on shelves or floors or nightstands*

BIBLIOTHECARY (noun, English)

one who collects, maintains, or cares for books

MAMIHLAPINATAPAI (noun, Yaghan)

*the look shared by two people who have reached an
unspoken understanding or who desire the same
thing but each wish that the other would offer it first*

STURMFREI (adjective, German)

lit. "stormfree"; the freedom of not being watched
by a parent or superior; being alone at home and
having the ability to do what you want

CWTCH (noun, Welsh)

a hug or a cuddle; a safe place; the space or
the cupboard under the stairs

ABDITORY (noun, English)

a place into which you can
disappear; a hiding place to preserve
the things that are most valued

RESFEBER (noun, c, Swedish)

*the restless race of the traveler's heart before the journey
begins, when anxiety and anticipation are tangled together;
a "travel fever" that can manifest as an illness*

FERNWEH (noun, n, German)

an ache for distant places; the craving for travel

SCHWELLENANGST

(noun, f, German)

lit. "threshold anxiety"; fear of embarking on something new or entering a place

DÉRIVE (noun, f, French and English)

lit. "drift"; a spontaneous journey where the traveler leaves ordinary life behind for a time to let the spirit of the landscape and architecture determine the path

ABLUVION (noun, English)
that which has been washed away

PARALIAN (noun, English)
one who lives by the sea

OFFING (noun, English)
the deep, distant stretch of the ocean that is still visible from the land; the foreseeable future

NEMOPHILIST (noun, English)
*a haunter of the woods; one who loves
the forest and its beauty and solitude*

PSITHURISM (noun, English)
the sound of the wind through the trees

RAÐLJÓST (noun, n, Icelandic)
enough light to find your way by

SMULTRONSTÄLLE (noun, c, Swedish)

lit. "place of wild strawberries"; a special place discovered,
treasured, returned to for solace and relaxation;
a personal idyll free from stress or sadness

UITWAAIEN (verb, Dutch)

to take a break and walk away from the demands of life to clear one's head

L'APPEL DU VIDE (noun phrase, French)

lit. "the call of the void"; the inexplicable draw of the dangerous and unknown future; the urge to throw oneself from safety into the gulf of an unexplored adventure, experience, or idea

HIRAETH (noun, m, Welsh)

a homesickness for a home to which you cannot return,
a home which maybe never was; the nostalgia,
the yearning, the grief for the lost places of your past

FUUBUTSUSHI (noun, Japanese)

the things—feelings, scents, images—that evoke
memories or anticipation of a particular season

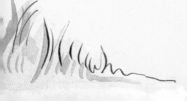

OBJETS TROUVÉS
(noun phrase, French and English)

*objects from nature or man-made objects past their
intended use, discovered again by chance, that have
a certain beauty about them*

KINTSUKUROI (noun, Japanese)

*lit. "to repair with gold"; the art of repairing pottery with
gold or silver lacquer and understanding that the piece is
more beautiful for having been broken*

SOIGNÉ (adjective, French and English)

*possessing an aura of sophistication in dress,
manner, or design; presented or prepared with an
elegance attained through care for the fine details*

NAZLANMAK (verb, Turkish)

*pretending reluctance or indifference when you are
actually willing and eager; saying no and meaning yes*

TARTLE (verb, Scots)

*to hesitate while introducing or meeting someone
because you have forgotten their name*

CROODLE (verb, English)

to cuddle or nestle together, from fear or cold;
to make a noise like a dove

INGLENOOK (noun, English)

a close, intimate corner by a fireplace where people
gather for warmth; from ingle, *a hearth (Scots)*

TACENDA (noun, English)

things better left unsaid; matters to be passed over in silence

MBUKI-MVUKI (verb phrase, Bantu)
*to shed one's clothing spontaneously and
dance naked in celebration*

BALTER (verb, English)
*to dance artlessly, without particular grace or
skill, but usually with enjoyment*

TARANTISM (noun, English)
*the uncontrollable urge to dance; overcoming
restlessness by getting up and dancing*

SITZFLEISCH (noun, n, German and English)

lit. "sitting flesh" or posterior; the ability to sit through, tolerate, or persist in something difficult or severely boring

AEOLIST (noun, English)

a blustering windbag of a person who only pretends to have inspiration or wisdom

NUNCHI (noun, Korean)

the subtle art of evaluating others' moods from their unspoken communications and knowing what not to say in a certain social situation

DEIPNOSOPHIST (noun, English)

someone skilled in small talk or in conversing around the dining table

ERLEBNISSE (noun, pl, n, German)

*the experiences, positive or negative, that we feel
most deeply, and through which we truly live;
not mere experiences, but Experiences*

SOBREMESA (noun, f, Spanish)

the time spent around the table after lunch or dinner
talking to the people with whom you shared the meal;
time to digest and savor both food and friendship

QUERENCIA (noun, f, Spanish)

a place from which one's strength is drawn,
where one feels at home; the place where you
are your most authentic self

GEZELLIG (adjective, Dutch)

cozy, nice, inviting, pleasant, comfortable;
connoting time spent with loved ones or togetherness
after a long separation

NYCTOPHILIA (noun, English)

*a love of darkness or night; finding relaxation
or comfort in the darkness*

CRYPTOSCOPOPHILIA (noun, English)

the urge to secretly peer through the
windows of homes as you pass by

SCINTILLA (noun, English)

a tiny, brilliant flash or spark; a small thing; a barely visible trace

PHOSPHENES (noun, English)

*the strange moving colors or "stars"
you see after you rub your eyes*

DORMIVEGLIA (noun, m, Italian)
the space that stretches between sleeping and waking

DWAAL (noun, South African English)
a dreaming, drifting, drowsy state;
(verb, Afrikaans) *to wander or stray as if one is dreaming*

RANTIPOLE (noun, English)

a wild, reckless young person;
(verb, English) *to be wild and reckless;*
(adjective, English) *wild and reckless*

NOCEUR (noun, m, French)

someone who goes to sleep late or not at all,
or one who stays out late to revel and party

SPHALLOLALIA (noun, English)

flirtatious talk that leads nowhere

BULBS

DIRL (verb, Scots and English)

to thrill, to vibrate; to tremble or quiver

FINIFUGAL (adjective, English)

*hating endings; of someone who tries to avoid or prolong
the final moments of a story, relationship, or some other journey*

CAFUNÉ (noun, m, Brazilian Portuguese)

running your fingers through the hair of someone you love

REDAMANCY (noun, English)

*the act of loving the one who loves you;
a love returned in full*

BY LANGUAGE

BANTU
mbuki-mvuki

BRAZILIAN PORTUGUESE
cafuné

DUTCH
gezellig
uitwaaien

ENGLISH
abditory
abluvion
aeolist
balter
bibliothecary
brontide
brumous
croodle
cryptoscopophilia
deipnosophist
dérive
dirl
finifugal
inglenook
jentacular
nemophilist
nyctophilia
objets trouvés
offing
oniochalasia
paralian
phosphenes
psithurism
rantipole
redamancy
scintilla
sitzfleisch
soigné
sphallolalia
tacenda
tarantism

FRENCH
dérive
l'appel du vide
noceur
objets trouvés
soigné

GERMAN
erlebnisse
fernweh
kummerspeck
schwellenangst
sitzfleisch
sturmfrei

ICELANDIC
hoppípolla
raðljóst

ITALIAN
dormiveglia

JAPANESE
fuubutsushi
honne
kintsukuroi
komorebi
tatemae
tsundoku

KOREAN
nunchi

PORTUGUESE
nefelibata

SCOTS
dirl
tartle

SOUTH AFRICAN ENGLISH
dwaal

SPANISH
nefelibata
querencia
sobremesa

SWEDISH
gökotta
resfeber
smultronställe

TURKISH
nazlanmak

WELSH
cwtch
hiraeth

YAGHAN
mamihlapinatapai

INDEX

NOTE: when a word's grammatical gender is noted, abbreviations mean: c—common, f—feminine, m—masculine, n—neuter

As a kid, **Yee-Lum Mak** loved long words best, but she's since learned
that lovely words come in many shapes. She lives in Los Angeles, California.

Kelsey Garrity-Riley grew up in Belgium and Germany before moving to the
United States to study illustration at the Savannah College of Art and Design.
She and her husband (who is also an illustrator) now call Brooklyn, New York, home.

To my brother and family, and to the authors
who taught me to love words
—Y. L. M.

To Mom, Dad, Collin, and Eliza,
& to Erik
you are my reference for the feelings of love
and the home that language struggles to define
—K. G. R.

Text copyright © 2016 by Yee-Lum Mak.
Illustrations copyright © 2016 by Kelsey Garrity-Riley.
All rights reserved. No part of this book may be reproduced
in any form without written permission from the publisher.

Library of Congress Cataloging-in-Publication Data:

Mak, Yee-Lum.
Other-Wordly : words both strange and lovely from around the world /
By Yee-Lum Mak, illustrated by Kelsey Garrity-Riley.
pages cm
ISBN 978-1-4521-2534-3
1. Language and languages—Foreign words and phrases.
2. Language and languages—Foreign elements.
3. Vocabulary—Influence on English. 1. Garrity-Riley, Kelsey, illustrator. II. Title.

P324.M35 2015
415—dc23

2014039037

Manufactured in China.

MIX
Paper from
responsible sources
FSC
www.fsc.org FSC™ C104723

Design by Kristine Brogno.
Typeset in Museo Sans and Georgia.
The illustrations in this book were rendered
in gouache, ink, and collage.

10 9 8 7 6 5 4 3 2 1

Chronicle Books LLC
680 Second Street
San Francisco, California 94107

Chronicle Books—we see things differently.
Become part of our community at www.chroniclekids.com.